I0409023

TABLE OF CONTENTS

INTRODUCTION

If you're anything like me, you've reached a point in life where you've had to stop and think about how dull and repetitive your life has become. Maybe you've reached that point of experiencing burnout from working your 9-to-5 or 12 hour shifts at work. You could even be a stay-at-home parent or single parent that just wants to be home with their children while making money. Whatever your reason may be, you just want the freedom to actually live and enjoy your life. This book is here to help!

This comprehensive guide is your roadmap to navigating the vast opportunities of the digital realm. Packed with practical advice, proven techniques, and real-world examples, the book will equip you with the knowledge and tools needed to embark on your online income journey. From e-commerce to freelancing, affiliate marketing to digital products, discover a wide range of methods and learn how to leverage the power of the internet to generate income, achieve flexibility, and unlock the lifestyle you desire and deserve. Get ready to embrace the digital revolution and unlock your potential for online success.

The potential of earning money online is truly remarkable and has revolutionized the way people can generate income. With the rapid advancement of technology and the increasing accessibility of the internet, opportunities to make money online have expanded exponentially. Here are some key reasons why earning money online holds immense potential:

- **Global Reach:** The internet connects the world creating a global marketplace. This means your potential customer base is not limited by geographical boundaries. Whether you offer products, services or content, you can reach a vast audience in markets that were previously inaccessible.
- **Flexibility and Convenience:** Online earning allows you to work from anywhere, at any time, as long as you have an internet connection. This freedom gives you the power to choose your own schedule, be your own boss, and achieve a desirable work-life balance. Online platforms provide the infrastructure to support your entrepreneurial aspirations.
- **Low Barrier to Entry:** Unlike traditional businesses that require substantial investments in physical infrastructure and inventory, online ventures can be launched with minimal upfront costs. Many online platforms provide user-friendly interfaces and tools that simplify the process of setting up an online presence. The barriers to entry are significantly lower, making it more accessible for individuals with diverse backgrounds and resources.
- **Diverse Monetization Methods:** The online world offers a myriad of ways to monetize your skills, knowledge, and creativity. You can create, promote, or offer services and products. Additionally, you can leverage social media platforms and content creation to generate ad revenue, sponsorships, or partnerships.

- **Scalability and Passive Income Potential:** Online businesses have the advantage of scalability, meaning you can grow your earnings exponentially without being limited by physical constraints. By automating certain processes, utilizing digital tools, and leveraging outsourcing, you can expand your online business and reach a larger audience without proportional increases in effort. Furthermore, certain online business models have the potential to generate passive income. This means that once the initial work is done, you can continue to earn money even when you're not actively working.

It's important to note that earning money online requires dedication, effort, and continuous learning. Success doesn't come overnight and it's crucial to choose legitimate opportunities and be wary of scams. Nonetheless, the potential for financial independence, flexibility, and a global reach makes earning money online an exciting and viable option for individuals looking to seize the opportunities of the digital age.

When reading a book about different methods of making money online, it's important to set realistic expectations to ensure a balanced understanding of the subject. Earning money online often involves acquiring new skills and knowledge. While some methods may be relatively straightforward to grasp, others can be more complex and require time and effort to master. Understand that there may be a learning curve involved and success may not come instantly. Patience, perseverance, and willingness to continuously learn and adapt are essential. The outcomes of online money-making methods can vary greatly from person to person. Factors such as individual effort, market demand, competition and timing can influence the level of success achieved. Approach each method with an open mind and adapt strategies based on personal circumstances and experiences.

Online ventures, like any business, carry inherent risks. It's crucial to be aware of potential pitfalls such as scams, fraudulent opportunities, or unsustainable business models. Exercise caution, conduct thorough research, and seek reputable sources of information before committing time, resources, or money to any money-making method. Building a sustainable online income typically requires persistence and adaptability, it may involve trial and error, experimentation, and willingness to adjust strategies based on market trends and feedback. Success often comes to those who are determined, resilient, and open to embracing new ideas and approaches.

Earning money online is not a get-rich-quick scheme. It requires consistent effort, hard work, and dedication. While certain methods may offer the potential for passive income or scalability, they usually involve an initial investment of time and energy to establish a solid foundation. Relying solely on a single money-making method can be risky. Diversifying your income streams by exploring various online opportunities can provide stability and reduce dependence on a single source of income. Exploring multiple methods also allows you to leverage different strengths, interests, and market niches. The online business landscape is dynamic and constantly evolving. Market trends, consumer behavior, and technology advancements can significantly impact the viability and profitability of various methods. Staying Informed, being adaptable, and continuously upgrading skills are crucial for long-term success.

CHAPTER ONE: UNDERSTANDING THE ONLINE LANDSCAPE

The rapid growth of the online economy can be attributed to several key factors that have converged to create a favorable environment for digital commerce. One key factor is internet penetration. The widespread availability and accessibility of the internet have played a crucial role in the expansion of the online economy. With more people gaining access to the internet through various devices like smartphones, tablets, and computers, the potential customer base for online businesses has significantly increased. The emergence of robust e-commerce platforms, such as Amazon, Alibaba, and eBay, has provided businesses and individuals with the infrastructure to set up online stores and reach a global customer base. These platforms offer user-friendly interfaces, secure payments gateways, and efficient logistics solutions, making it easier for sellers to enter the online market.

Online shopping offers unparalleled convenience and access. Consumers can browse and purchase products or services from the comfort of their homes or on the go, eliminating the need for physical travel to brick-and-mortar stores.

The 24/7 availability of online businesses allows customers to shop at any time that suits them, which is a significant advantage over traditional retail. As mentioned before, the internet offers a global reach giving small and medium-sized enterprises (SMEs) a customer base on a global scale. Additionally, advancements in logistics and shipping have made it easier and more cost-effective to deliver products to customers internationally.

Cost efficiency is another key factor in the rapid growth of the online economy. For businesses, operating online often involves lower overhead costs compared to maintaining a physical store. Online businesses can avoid expenses associated with rent, utilities, and staffing. This cost efficiency enables entrepreneurs to start and scale their ventures more easily. Marketing is a major key factor and the internet makes that much easier. The online economy offers advanced targeting and personalized marketing capabilities, allowing businesses to tailor their advertising and promotions to specific demographics and customer preferences. This personalized approach enhances the customer experience, increases engagement, and drives conversions. Data analytics and tracking tools provide valuable insights that enable businesses to refine their marketing strategies further.

Rapid advancements in technology have played a significant role in the growth of the online economy. Innovations such as mobile payment systems, artificial intelligence, data analytics, and cloud computing have made online transactions more secure, efficient, and seamless. These technologies have also facilitated the development of new business models and marketplaces.

Consumer behavior has contributed to the growth of the online economy. It has evolved significantly, with more people embracing online shopping and digital services. The convenience, wider product selection, competitive pricing, and personalized experiences offered by online retailers have contributed to the shift. The COVID-19 pandemic further accelerated the adoption of online shopping as people sought to minimize physical contact and adhere to social distancing measures.

Overall, the rapid growth of the online economy can be attributed to a combination of technological advancements, changing consumer behavior, increased accessibility, and the cost efficiency of digital commerce. As these factors continue to evolve and improve, we can expect further expansion and innovation in the online economy. Making money online offers several advantages that have contributed to its popularity as a viable income-generating option.

One of the major advantages of making money online is the flexibility it provides. Online work allows individuals to set their own schedules and work from anywhere. This flexibility is particularly beneficial for those lacking a work-life balance in their current employment or have personal commitments that require flexible working arrangements. Minimal to none startup costs reduce financial barriers, making the online economy a more appealing option for income, as well.

Making money online offers a wide range of income streams and monetization options. Individuals can choose from various online business models such as, e-commerce, freelancing, digital products, affiliate marketing, content creation, online consulting, and more.

This diversity allows individuals to explore multiple avenues and diversify their income sources, reducing dependence on a single source of revenue. With the right strategies and execution, it is possible to expand an online venture rapidly. Digital products, online courses and software solutions, for example, can be replicated and sold to an ever-expanding customer base without significant additional costs. This scalability enables individuals to maximize their earnings and achieve substantial growth.

To successfully make money online, certain mindsets and skills are crucial. Adopting an entrepreneurial mindset is essential for online success . This involves having a proactive and opportunity-driven approach, being willing to take calculated risks, and embracing innovation and adaptability. Online entrepreneurs need to be self-motivated, persistent, and resilient in the face of challenges and setbacks. Working online requires self-discipline and effective time management. Without the structure of a traditional office environment, it's important to set clear goals, prioritize tasks, and manage time effectively. Establishing routines, setting deadlines, and avoiding distractions are essential to maintain focus and productivity.

The online landscape is constantly evolving, so a mindset of continuous learning is needed. Successful online earners stay updated with the latest trends, tools and techniques relevant to their field. They invest time in acquiring new skills, improving existing ones, and staying ahead of the competition. Embracing a growth mindset and seeking out educational resources, online courses, and communities can help in this regard. An important skill to have is digital literacy.

Being digitally literate is essential for making money online. It involves having a solid understanding of internet technologies, online platforms, and digital tools relevant to your chosen field. Basic knowledge of website creation, social media platforms, digital marketing, search engine optimization (SEO), data analytics, and online security is beneficial.

To be a successful online earner, you must possess marketing and sales skills to effectively promote your products or services. Understanding the principles of marketing, branding, and customer psychology is crucial for attracting and engaging online audiences. Skills like copywriting, content creation, social media marketing, email marketing, and search engine marketing (SEM) can contribute to effective promotion conversion. Building a strong online network and fostering relationships within your industry or niche is vital, as well. Engaging with other professionals, influencers, and potential customers through social media, online communities, and forums can lead to collaborations, partnerships, and valuable opportunities. Networking can help increase visibility, gain insights, and open doors for growth and monetization.

The online landscape is highly dynamic, and successful online earners are adaptable and agile. They embrace changes, pivot when necessary, and are quick to capitalize on emerging opportunities. Being open to new ideas, feedback, and customer insights allows for constant refinement and improvement of online offerings. Putting the customer at the center of your online activities is essential. Understanding their needs, preferences, and pain points enables you to create valuable products or services. Active listening, gathering feedback, and providing excellent customer support are key components of a customer-centric approach.

Making money online requires effective financial management. This involves tracking income, expenses, and profit margins, as well as budgeting and planning for future growth, Understanding pricing strategies, profit models, and financial metrics helps in making informed decisions and optimizing profitability. Setbacks and challenges are inevitable when making money online. Resilience and perseverance are essential to your success as an online earner. Refuse to give up in the face of obstacles. Learn from failures, adjust strategies, and stay focused on your long-term goals.

Remember, while these mindsets and skills are important, they can be developed and honed over time. It's essential to be proactive, seek knowledge, and take consistent action to increase your chances of success in the online space.

CHAPTER TWO: FREELANCING AND REMOTE WORK

Freelancing refers to a form of work where individuals, often referred to as freelancers or independent contractors, offer their services to clients on a project-by-project basis. Instead of being employed by a single company, freelancers work independently and typically have multiple clients at any given time. They have the freedom to choose the projects they work on, set their own rates and working hours, and often have the flexibility to work from anywhere they choose.

Remote work, on the other hand, refers to a work arrangement where employees or freelancers perform their job duties outside of a traditional office environment, Instead of commuting to a physical workplace, remote workers use technology and communication tools to carry out their tasks from a location of their choice, which can be their home, a coworking space, or any other place with internet connection.

Remote work is closely associated with the advancement of technology and the availability of digital tools that enable effective communication, collaboration, and productivity. It has gained significant popularity in recent years, offering numerous benefits such as increased flexibility, reduced commuting time, access to a global talent pool, and improved work-life balance.

While freelancing and remote work are distinct concepts, they often overlap. Many freelancers choose to work remotely, taking advantage of the flexibility and autonomy that remote work provides. Additionally, remote employees working for a company may also be considered freelancers if they are hired on a contractual basis rather than as full-time employees.

Here are some popular freelancing platforms where individuals can find work opportunities or hire freelancers for various projects:

- **Upwork:** Upwork is one of the largest freelancing platforms, offering a wide range of job categories, including writing, design, programming, marketing, and more. It provides a user-friendly interface, allows freelancers to create profiles, and connects them with clients through a bidding system.
- **Fiverr:** Fiverr is known for its gig-based system, where freelancers offer specific services, referred to as "gigs", for a set price starting at $5. It covers a broad spectrum of creative and professional services, such as graphic design, copywriting, video editing, and social media management.
- **Freelancer:** Freelancer is a global platform that connects freelancers with clients seeking services across various industries. It offers a bidding system, skills tests, and an extensive job category list that includes programming, writing, marketing, design, and more.

- **Toptal:** Toptal is a platform that focuses on connecting clients with top-tier freelancers in the fields of software development, design, and finance. Toptal has a rigorous screening process to ensure that freelancers have exceptional skills and experience.
- **Guru:** Guru is a freelancing platform that covers a wide range of job categories, including writing, design, programming, and more. It provides features such as workrooms for collaboration, a work agreement system, and a secure payment platform.
- **PeoplePerHour:** PeoplePerHour is a platform that specializes in freelance work within the creative, marketing, and programming fields. It allows freelancers to showcase their skills and set hourly or project-based rates. Clients can post job offers or search for freelancers directly.
- **99designs:** 99designs is a platform specifically for graphic designers. It operates on a contest-based model where clients post design projects, and designers submit their work. The client then selects the winning design and pays the designer a pre-determined fee.

These are just a few examples of popular freelancing platforms available. It's important to note that each platform has its own unique features, fee structures, and user base, so it's beneficial to explore multiple platforms and find the one that best suits your needs as a freelancer or a client.

Freelance work encompasses a wide range of skills and industries. Writing and editing are a couple of in-demand skills in areas such as content writing, copywriting, blogging, and proofreading. To get started, develop a portfolio of writing samples, showcase your expertise on platforms like Medium or a personal blog, and join freelancing platforms specific to writing, such as Upwork or Freelancer.

Graphic design is a skill that involves creating visual content for digital or print media, including logos, marketing materials, illustrations, and website design. Build a strong portfolio showcasing your design skills, learn popular design tools like Adobe Photoshop or Illustrator, and utilize platforms like Behance or Dribbble to showcase your work and attract clients.

Web development is another freelancing skill that involves building and maintaining websites. Learn programming languages like HTML, CSS, and JavaScript, and gain proficiency in popular frameworks such as Word Press or React. Create a portfolio website to showcase your skills and leverage freelancing platforms like Upwork or Toptal to find web developing projects.

Digital marketing is a skill in high demand in areas such as search engine optimization (SEO), social media management, pay-per-click (PPC) advertising, and email marketing. Stay updated with industry trends, take online courses or certifications in digital marketing (can be done for free through The American Dream Academy), and build a portfolio showcasing your successful campaigns. Platforms like Upwork, Freelancer, or PeoplePerHour offer digital marketing job opportunities.

If you are proficient in multiple languages, translation and language services can be a lucrative freelance skill. Specialize in specific industries or language pairs, obtain relevant certifications if available, and join translation focused platforms like TranslatorsCafe or ProZ for job opportunities.

With the rise of video content, skills in video production, shooting, and editing are in demand. Learn video editing software like Adobe Premiere Pro or Final Cut Pro, practice your video production skills, and create a portfolio showcasing your work. Platforms like Upwork, Fiverr, or Freelancer offer opportunities in video production and editing.

To get started in freelance work, consider the following steps:

1. **Define your niche**: Identify your specific skills and target industries where you can provide value.
2. **Build a portfolio**: Create a portfolio showcasing your best work to demonstrate your skills and attract clients. If you don't have previous freelance work, consider creating sample projects or collaborating with friends or non-profit organizations.
3. **Set up an online presence**: Create a professional website or use platforms like LinkedIn, Behance, or GitHub to showcase your skills and portfolio. Optimize your profiles with relevant keywords and showcase your expertise.
4. **Network:** Network within your industry by attending relevant events, joining professional groups, or engaging with online communities. Building relationships can lead to referrals and potential clients.

5.**Utilize freelancing platforms:** Sign up for popular freelancing platforms, such as the platforms mentioned previously, to find projects. Create a compelling profile, set competitive rates, and apply for relevant projects.

6.**Deliver quality work:** Focus on delivering high-quality work to build a reputation and receive positive reviews and recommendations from clients. Satisfied clients can become repeat customers or provide referrals.

7.**Continuous learning and improvement:** Stay updated with industry trends, technologies, and best practices. Invest in learning new skills, taking relevant courses, or obtaining certifications to enhance your expertise and stay competitive.

Building a strong freelancing profile and attracting clients is crucial for success in the freelance industry. Use a high-quality, professional-looking profile picture that reflects your brand and creates a positive first impression. Create a headline that highlights your key skills, expertise, and value proposition. Make it concise and attention-grabbing to capture the interest of potential clients. Your profile's introduction or summary should provide a clear and concise overview of your skills, experience, and what you can offer clients. Focus on highlighting your unique selling points and how you can solve their problems or meet their needs.

Include a portfolio section in your profile that showcases your best work. Select a variety of high-quality samples that demonstrate your skills and expertise. If you don't have previous work, create personal projects or collaborate with others to build your portfolio. Make sure to clearly list your skills, areas of expertise, and any relevant certifications or qualifications. Be specific and include keywords that clients might search for when looking for freelancers with your skills.

If you have done previous work for clients and have received positive feedback or testimonials, include them in your profile. Actively seek recommendations and referrals by reaching out to previous clients for feedback or testimonials to add to your profile. Testimonials provide social proof and build trust with potential clients. Research market rates for your skills and set your rates accordingly. Consider starting with competitive rates to attract clients initially and gradually increase them as you gain experience and positive reviews.

Incorporate relevant keywords throughout your profile to increase visibility in search results. Think about the terms clients might use when searching for freelancers in your field and incorporate them naturally in your profile.Clearly describe the services you offer, your process, and what clients can expect when working with you. Specificity helps clients understand how you can meet their needs and sets clear expectations from the start. Regularly update your profile with new work samples, skills, certifications, or any noteworthy achievements. An updated profile demonstrates your commitment to your craft and keeps it fresh for potential clients.

Always provide exceptional customer service. When you start working with clients, go the extra mile. Satisfied clients are more likely to provide reviews and refer you to others. Lastly, engage with the freelancing community. Participate in online forums, groups, or communities related to your field. Engaging with other freelancers and sharing your expertise can help establish your credibility and attract clients.

Building a strong profile takes time and effort. Continuously refine and update your profile based on client feedback and market trends. Be proactive in marketing yourself, and consistently deliver high-quality work to establish a strong reputation and attract clients to your freelancing business. Starting on freelance work requires dedication, persistence, and continuous improvement. As you gain experience and build a solid reputation, you can expand your client base and potentially increase your rates over time.

CHAPTER THREE: E-COMMERCE AND DROPSHIPPING

E-commerce, short for electronic commerce, refers to the buying and selling of goods and services over the internet. It involves online transactions, where customers browse products or services on websites or mobile applications and make purchases using electronic payment methods. E-commerce has revolutionized the way businesses operate and how people engage in commercial activities.

The potential of e-commerce is vast and continues to grow rapidly. E-commerce transcends geographical boundaries, enabling businesses to reach customers anywhere in the world. It eliminates the limitations of physical stores and allows businesses to tap into international markets with ease. This global reach opens up immense opportunities for expansion and growth. E-commerce offers convenience to both businesses and customers. Shoppers can browse and purchase products or services at any time. Businesses can operate 24/7 without the constraints of traditional store hours. This accessibility enhances the overall customer experience and increases sales potential.

Operating through e-commerce reduces many costs you would have in a physical store, such as rent and utilities. Additionally, automation and streamlined processes reduce operational costs, inventory management, and order fulfillment expenses. E-commerce platforms collect vast amounts of customer data, allowing businesses to analyze and understand their customers better. This data can be used to create targeted marketing campaigns, personalized product recommendations, and tailored shopping experiences. By delivering relevant content and offers, businesses can increase customer engagement and drive sales.

Online stores can easily accommodate growth by expanding product catalogs, adding more server capacity, and integrating new technologies. E-commerce platforms also offer flexibility in adapting to changing market trends and customer preferences, enabling businesses to stay agile and competitive. These platforms enable businesses to gather valuable insights into customer behavior, preferences, and purchasing patterns. This information helps businesses make data-driven decisions, improve product offerings, optimize pricing strategies, and enhance customer service. By understanding their customers better, businesses can build stronger relationships and foster customer loyalty.

E-commerce continues to evolve by incorporating emerging technologies such as artificial intelligence (AI) and virtual reality (VR). These technologies enhance the online shopping experience by providing personalized recommendations, virtual try-on experiences, interactive product visualization, and chatbot-powered customer support.

In conclusion, e-commerce offers immense potential for businesses to expand their reach, increase revenue, and improve customer experiences. It has transformed the way people buy and sell products and services. With ongoing enhancements in technology and evolving consumer expectations, e-commerce is poised to play an increasingly significant role in the global economy.

The dropshipping model is a business model where an online retailer (the dropshipper) sells products to customers without physically storing or handling the inventory. Instead, the dropshipper partners with a supplier or manufacturer who handles the inventory storage, packaging, and shipment of products directly to the customers.

Here's how the dropshipping model works:

- **Setting up an Online Store:** The dropshipper establishes an online store, either through their website or a third-party e-commerce platform. They curate a selection of products from the supplier's catalog to display in their store.
- **Product Selection and Listing:** The dropshipper selects the products they want to sell from the supplier's inventory. They obtain product descriptions, images, and prices from the supplier and create product listings on their online store. These listings should accurately represent the products and provide all necessary information for customers.
- **Customer Places an Order:** When a customer visits the dropshipper's online store and places an order, the dropshipper receives the order details, including the customer's shipping address and payment information.

- **Order Forwarding to the Supplier:** The dropshipper then forwards the order and the corresponding payment to the supplier. The supplier processes the order and prepares the product for shipment.
- **Shipment and Delivery:** The supplier packages and ships the product directly to the customer's address provided by the dropshipper. The packaging usually doesn't include any branding or information that would reveal the involvement of the supplier.
- **Order Tracking and Customer Support:** The dropshipper tracks the shipment and provides the customer with the relevant tracking information. If the customer has any questions or issues regarding the order, the dropshipper handles the customer support and acts as the primary point of contact.
- **Profit and Margins:** The dropshipper earns profit from the difference between the price at which they sell the product to the customer and the price at which they purchase the product from the supplier. The dropshipper sets their own prices, taking into account factors such as supplier costs, marketing expenses, and desired profit margins.

The dropshipping model has some key benefits. Dropshipping eliminates the need for upfront inventory investment, as the dropshipper only purchases products from the supplier when a customer places an order. This reduces the initial capital required to start the business. Setting up an online store and listing products is relatively straightforward, especially with the availability of e-commerce platforms and tools. Dropshipping simplifies the logistics of inventory management, order fulfillment, and shipping since these tasks are handled by the supplier.

It also allows businesses to easily scale their operations by adding more products to their catalog without the need for additional storage space or logistics infrastructure. Dropshippers can offer a wide variety of products from different suppliers, providing customers with a broader range of options.

While the dropshipping model offers various advantages, it's important to note that it also has challenges. These include intense competition, lower profit margins compared to traditional retail, reliance on the supplier's inventory management and shipping efficiency, and potential issues with product quality control and customer satisfaction if the supplier doesn't meet expectations. Overall, dropshipping can be a viable business model for entrepreneurs looking to start an online retail venture with minimal upfront costs and logistical complexities.

There are several popular e-commerce platforms available that offer a range of features and functionalities to help set up and manage an online store. Let's discuss a few of the prominent ones:

- **Shopify:** Shopify is one of the most widely used e-commerce platforms, known for its user-friendly interface and extensive app store. It provides a comprehensive solution for building and managing an online store. With Shopify, you can choose from a variety of customizable themes, set up product listings, manage inventory, process payments, and track orders. It also offers integration with various third-party apps and supports dropshipping.

- **WooCommerce:** WooCommerce is a popular e-commerce plugin for WordPress, making it an excellent choice if you already have a WordPress website. It provides a robust set of features to turn your website into an e-commerce store. With WooCommerce, you can manage product listings, set up payment gateways, handle inventory, and customize the store's appearance using themes and extensions. It offers flexibility and scalability, allowing you to expand your store's functionality as needed.
- **Magento:** Magento is a feature-rich e-commerce platform that caters to businesses of all sizes, from small startups to large enterprises. It offers a high level of customization and scalability, making it suitable for complex e-commerce requirements. Magento provides a wide range of features such as advanced product management, flexible pricing options, multi-store capabilities, and strong SEO capabilities. However, it requires technical expertise to set up and manage effectively.
- **BigCommerce:** BigCommerce is a fully hosted e-commerce platform that offers a comprehensive set of features for creating and managing an online store. It provides a user-friendly interface, customizable themes, and various built-in marketing tools. BigCommerce supports a wide range of payment gateways, offers inventory management, and integrates with popular marketplaces like Amazon and eBay. It is known for its scalability and performance, making it suitable for growing businesses.

To set up an online store using these platforms, here's a general step-by-step process:

1. **Sign up and Choose a Plan:** Visit the website of your chosen e-commerce platform and sign up for an account. Select an appropriate pricing plan based on your business needs and budget.
2. **Select a Domain Name:** Choose a domain name for your online store that is unique and represents your brand. If you don't have a domain, most platforms offer the option to purchase one directly from them or integrate with third-party domain providers.
3. **Customize the Store's Appearance:** Select a theme or template provided by the platform and customize it to match your branding. Customize the layout, colors, fonts, and other visual elements to create a unique and visually appealing store.
4. **Set Up Product Listings:** Add products to your store by providing detailed descriptions. Images, pricing, and other relevant information. Organize products into categories or collections for easy navigation.
5. **Configure Payment Gateways:** Set up payment gateways to enable customers to make secure online transactions. Popular options include PayPal, Stripe, and various credit card processors. Configure shipping options and rates based on your preferences and location.
6. **Configure Store Settings:** Adjust various store settings, including tax settings, inventory management, shipping options, and order fulfillment preferences.
7. **Test and Launch:** Before launching your store, thoroughly test its functionality. Including the checkout process, payment gateway integration, and responsiveness across different devices. Make any necessary adjustments or improvements based on the test results.

8.**Promote Your Store:** Once your store is live, focus on driving traffic and promoting your products. Utilize digital marketing techniques such as search engine optimization (SEO), social media marketing, email marketing, and content marketing to attract visitors and convert them into customers.

Remember that each e-commerce platform has its own specific setup process and features. Consult the platform's documentation and resources for detailed instructions on how to operate their platform to your full advantage.

Product selection, marketing, and customer service are essential components of starting a successful dropshipping business. Here are some helpful tips:

Product Selection:

- Conduct market research to identify popular product categories, trending items, and customer demands. Look for products with a good balance of demand and competition to maximize your chances of success.
- Consider focusing on a specific niche or target market. By catering to a specific audience, you can differentiate yourself from competitors and build a loyal customer base.
- Choose reliable suppliers who offer high-quality products and fast shipping. Read reviews, request samples, and ensure that the products meet your standards. Quality products contribute to customer satisfaction and help build a positive reputation for your business.

- Analyze the pricing strategies of your competitors and set competitive prices for your products. Consider factors like supplier costs, shipping fees, and desired profit margins. Offering competitive prices can attract customers and increase your chances of making sales.

Marketing:

- Build a strong online presence. Invest in creating a professional and visually appealing website or online store. Optimize your website for search engines and ensure it is mobile-friendly. Leverage social media platforms, content marketing, and paid advertising to drive traffic to your store.
- Create valuable and engaging content related to your products and niche. This can include blog articles, product guides, tutorials, or videos. Content marketing helps establish your expertise, attracts organic traffic, and builds trust with potential customers.
- Utilize social media platforms to promote your products and engage with your target audience. Create engaging content, run targeted ads, collaborate with influencers, and actively respond to customer inquiries and comments.
- Build an email list and develop email marketing campaigns to nurture customer relationships. Send out newsletters, exclusive offers, and personalized recommendations to keep customers engaged and encourage repeat purchases.

Customer Service:

- Respond to customer inquiries and concerns promptly and professionally. Provide multiple channels for customer support, such as email, live chat, or social media messaging. Quick and helpful responses enhance the customer experience and build trust.
- Keep customers informed about the status of their orders through order tracking. Send regular updates on order fulfillment, shipping delays, or any other relevant information. Proactive communication shows that you care about customer satisfaction.
- Establish a clear and customer-friendly return and refund policy. Make the process as seamless as possible for customers who may need to return or exchange products. This helps build trust and confidence in your business.
- Implement personalization techniques in your communication with customers. Address them by their names, recommend related products based on their purchase history, and follow up after a purchase to ensure their satisfaction. Personalized interactions enhance the customer experience and increase the likelihood of repeat business.

Remember, providing an excellent customer experience is crucial for the success of your dropshipping or e-commerce business. Continuously monitor customer feedback, adapt your strategies accordingly, and aim to exceed customer expectations at every touchpoint.

CHAPTER FOUR: AFFILIATE MARKETING

Affiliate marketing is a performance-based marketing model where an individual or business (the affiliate) promotes products or services of another company (the merchant) in exchange for a commission on successful sales or desired action generated through their marketing efforts. It operates on the principle of revenue sharing, where affiliates earn a portion of the revenue they help generate for the merchant.

Affiliate marketing is typically a simple process. Affiliates join an affiliate program or network by signing up with the merchant or a dedicated affiliate platform. They provide their information and agree to the terms and conditions of the program. Affiliates then choose the products or services they want to promote from the merchant's offerings. They may have access to a range of promotional materials such as unique affiliate links, banners, product images, and marketing content.

Once products or services are selected, an affiliate will promote and market the products or services. Affiliates use various marketing channels and strategies to promote the merchant's products or services. This can include creating content on websites or blogs, sharing affiliate links on social media, running paid advertising campaigns, or utilizing email marketing. Affiliates use unique links provided by the merchant or affiliate network to track their marketing efforts. These links typically contain a specific identifier that associates the sales or actions generated with the respective affiliate.

When a customer clicks on an affiliate's unique link and completes a desired action (such as making a purchase, filling out a form, or subscribing to a service), the affiliate's tracking link captures the information. The merchant's tracking system attributes the conversion to the corresponding affiliate and records the sale or action. The merchant calculates the commission earned by each affiliate based on the agreed-upon commission structure (e.g., a percentage of the sale value or fixed amount per action). The merchant usually holds a specific period for order validation and ensures that the sales or actions are legitimate before approving the commissions. Both the merchant and the affiliate have access to reporting and analytics tools provided by the affiliate program or network. These tools track and report key metrics such as clicks, conversions, sales, and commissions. They help affiliates analyze their performance and optimize their marketing strategies accordingly.

Affiliate marketing offers several benefits for all participants involved. Merchants leverage the marketing efforts of affiliates to expand their reach and increase sales, while affiliates can monetize their online presence and audience by promoting relevant products. Customers also benefit from the recommendations and insights provided by affiliates, which can help them make informed purchasing decisions. Overall, affiliate marketing provides a win-win situation, allowing merchants to gain exposure and generate sales while rewarding affiliates for their marketing efforts and driving revenue.

Choosing profitable niches and products is a crucial step in building a successful affiliate marketing business. Here are some factors to consider when selecting profitable niches and products:

- **Research Market Demand:** Start by conducting market research to identify niches and products with high demand. Look for trends, popular products, and emerging markets. Use tools like Google Trends, keyword search tools, and market research reports to gather insights on search volume, consumer interests, and competition.
- **Assess Competition:** Evaluate the level of competition in your chosen niche. While some competition is healthy and indicates market demand, too much competition can make it challenging to differentiate your business. Look for underserved sub-niches or find unique selling points that set you apart from competitors.
- **Target Audience and Buyer Persona:** Understand your target audience and their needs. Define your ideal customer by creating a buyer persona. Identify their demographics, interests, pain points, and purchasing

behavior. Choose niches and products that align with your target audience's preferences and have the potential to solve their problems or fulfill their desires.

- **Profit Margins:** Consider the profit potential of the products you intend to sell. Evaluate the cost of sourcing or manufacturing the products, including any associated fees such as shipping or packaging costs. Compare the costs with the expected selling price to ensure reasonable profit margins that sustain your business.
- **Seasonality and Long-Term Viability:** Assess whether the niche or product is subject to seasonality if it has long-term viability. Seasonal products can be profitable during specific periods, but you may need to diversify your offerings or target other niches during off-seasons. Look for niches and products that have a consistent demand throughout the year.
- **Product Differentiation and Unique Value Proposition (UVP):** Determine how you can differentiate yourself in the market. Identify unique features, benefits, or selling points that make your products stand out from the competition. This could include factors such as product quality, design functionality, customer service, or exclusive offerings.
- **Supplier Reliability and Product Quality:** Choose reliable suppliers or manufacturers who can consistently provide high-quality products. Read reviews, request product samples, and evaluate the supplier's track record in terms of order fulfillment, shipping times, and customer satisfaction. Ensuring product quality is crucial for customer satisfaction and maintaining a positive reputation.
- **Scalability and Upselling Opportunities:** Consider the potential for scaling your business and the availability of

related products or upselling opportunities within the niche. Having a range of complementary products or the ability to expand your product offerings can help increase customer lifetime value and maximize profitability.

- **Personal Interest and Passion:** While not a prerequisite, having a personal interest or passion for the niche or products you choose can provide additional motivation and enjoyment in running your business. It can also help you better understand your target audience and make informed decisions.

Continuous market research, monitoring consumer trends, and adapting to changing demands are essential for long-term success. Regularly evaluate and refine your niche and product selection based on market feedback and data analysis to stay profitable and relevant in the ever-evolving e-commerce landscape.

There are numerous affiliate networks and platforms available, each with its own features, commission structures, and industry focuses. Here are some of the popular ones:

- **Amazon Associates:** Amazon Associates is one of the largest and most well-known affiliate programs. It allows affiliates to promote a wide range of products available on Amazon and earn commissions on qualifying purchases. With vast product selection and trusted brand reputation, Amazon Associates attracts affiliates across various niches.
- **Commission Junction (CJ Affiliate):** CJ Affiliate is a widely recognized affiliate network that offers a diverse range of affiliate programs from well-known brands and

advertisers. It provides access to a large number of advertisers across various industries, enabling affiliates to find suitable products and services to promote.

- **ShareASale:** ShareASale is a well-established affiliate network that features a wide range of merchants and products. It offers a user-friendly interface, robust reporting and tracking tools, and a variety of promotional options. ShareASale covers a broad range of niches, making it suitable for affiliates with different interests.
- **Rakuten Advertising:** Rakuten Advertising (formerly LinkShare) is a global affiliate network that connects affiliates with merchants worldwide. It offers a comprehensive suite of tools, including advanced tracking, reporting, and commission management. Rakuten Advertising provides opportunities to promote products across various industries and geographic regions.
- **ClickBank:** ClickBank is an affiliate marketplace primarily focused on digital products, such as e-books, online courses, software, and memberships. It is known for its high commission rates and easy-to-use platform. ClickBank's marketplace features a wide range of products in various niches, attracting affiliates interested in digital content.
- **Awin:** Awin is a global affiliate network that operates in multiple countries and industries. It offers a diverse range of advertisers and provides affiliates with access to exclusive campaigns, advanced reporting, and performance tracking tools. Awin caters to affiliates and advertisers seeking international reach and localization options.

- **Impact:** Impact (formerly Impact Radius) is an affiliate marketing platform that offers an all-in-one solution for managing affiliate programs. It provides features such as tracking, reporting, commission management, and partner recruitment. Impact serves various industries and supports both traditional and influencer-based affiliate marketing models.
- **FlexOffers:** FlexOffers is an affiliate network that connects affiliates with a wide range of advertisers and merchants. It offers a vast selection of affiliate programs across diverse industries and provides tools for tracking, reporting, and optimizing campaigns. FlexOffers focuses on providing affiliates with flexible options to monetize their online presence.

These are just a few examples of the many affiliate networks and platforms available. When choosing an affiliate network or platform, consider factors such as the range of available advertisers, commission structures, payment methods, reporting capabilities, and support services. It's also essential to review the terms and conditions of each network or platform to ensure they align with your business goals and marketing strategies.

To attract traffic, optimize conversions, and earn commissions in affiliate marketing, consider implementing the following strategies:
- **Content Marketing:** Create high-quality and informative content that is relevant to the products or services you are promoting. This can include blog posts, articles, tutorials, product reviews, or comparison guides. Optimize your content for search engines to increase organic traffic and leverage keywords that align with your target audience's search intent.

- **Search Engine Optimization (SEO):** Optimize your website or blog for search engines by implementing SEO best practices. Focus on keyword research, on-page optimization (such as meta tags, headings, and keyword-rich content), and building backlinks from authoritative sources. Higher search engine rankings can drive organic traffic and increase the visibility of your affiliate links.
- **Social Media Marketing:** Utilize social media platforms to promote your affiliate products and engage with your audience. Create compelling content, including images, videos, and captions that highlight the benefits or solutions provided by the products. Engage with your followers, respond to comments, and actively participate in relevant communities or groups to expand your reach.
- **Email Marketing:** Build an email list of interested subscribers and develop email marketing campaigns to nurture relationships and promote affiliate products. Send regular newsletters, exclusive offers, or personalized recommendations to your subscribers. Segment your email list based on interests or previous purchases to provide more targeted and relevant content.
- **Influencer Partnerships:** Collaborate with influencers or bloggers who have an established audience and credibility in your niche. Engage in sponsored posts, guest blogging, or product reviews to leverage their influence and reach. This can help drive traffic to your affiliate links and increase conversions through their recommendations.

- **Paid Advertising:** Consider running paid advertising campaigns to drive targeted traffic to your affiliate offers. Platforms like Google Ads, social media advertising (such as Facebook Ads or Instagram Ads), or native advertising networks can be effective in reaching your target audience. However, ensure that your advertising costs align with your expected commissions and maintain a positive return on investment (ROI).
- **Conversion Rate Optimization (CRO):** Continuously analyze and optimize your website or landing pages to improve conversion rates. Utilize A/B testing to experiment with different layouts, calls to action, or copywriting techniques. Optimize page load times, mobile responsiveness, and user experience to enhance conversions and reduce bounce rates.
- **Trust and Authority Building:** Build trust and establish yourself as an authority in your niche. Provide valuable and reliable information, be transparent about your affiliations, and only promote products you genuinely believe in. Share testimonials, user reviews, or case studies to demonstrate the effectiveness and credibility of the products you promote.
- **Track and Analyze Data:** Utilize tracking tools and analytics to monitor the performance of your affiliate marketing campaigns. Track clicks, conversions, and earnings to identify what strategies are working best for you. Use the data to refine your marketing efforts, optimize your campaigns, and focus on the most profitable products or channels.

Success in affiliate marketing, like other online businesses, takes time, effort, and continuous refinement of your strategies. It's crucial to understand your target audience, provide value, and maintain transparency to build trust and maximize your commissions. Regularly analyze your results, adapt your approaches, and stay updated with industry trends to stay ahead in the competitive affiliate marketing landscape.

CHAPTER FIVE: DIGITAL PRODUCTS AND ONLINE COURSES

The demand for digital products and online courses has experienced significant growth in recent years. This trend accelerated even further by the global COVID-19 pandemic, which forced people to stay at home and seek alternative ways to learn, work, and entertain themselves.

Digital products and online courses offer accessibility to a wide range of audiences. People from different locations and backgrounds can access educational content and resources without geographical limitations. Online courses enable individuals to learn at their own pace and convenience, eliminating barriers to education and professional development. Online courses and digital products provide flexibility and convenience to learners. They can access materials, modules, and resources at any time and from any location with an internet connection. This flexibility is particularly attractive to individuals with busy schedules or those who prefer self-paced learning.

Digital products and online courses often offer a more cost-effective alternative compared to traditional in-person education or physical products. Online courses are typically more affordable than attending physical classes or workshops, making education and skill development accessible to a broader audience. Additionally, digital products, such as e-books or software, eliminate production and distribution costs associated with physical goods. The digital landscape provides a vast array of online courses covering various subjects, industries, and skill sets. Learners can choose from a wide range of topics and find courses tailored to their specific needs and interests. This diversity of options enables individuals to explore new areas of knowledge, enhance their existing skills, or pivot their careers.

The demand for lifelong learning has increased as industries evolve rapidly and new technologies emerge. Online courses offer individuals the opportunity to continuously upgrade their skills and stay competitive in the job market. Digital products, such as e-books, webinars, or podcasts, also contribute to ongoing personal and professional development. The advancements in technology, particularly the internet, have paved the way for digital products and online courses. High-speed internet connectivity, the proliferation of mobile devices, and the rise of e-learning platforms have made accessing digital products and online courses easier than ever before.

The demand for digital products and online courses has grown due to their accessibility, flexibility, cost-effectiveness, diverse learning options, continuous skill development opportunities, technological advancements, and the rise of remote work and remote learning. These factors indicate the increasing preferences for digital solutions in various aspects of education, personal development, and professional growth.

There are various types of digital products that can be created, each with its own unique creation process. Here are a few examples of digital products and an overview of their creation processes:

1. **E-books:**

- **Idea Generation:** Determine the topic or subject of the e-book based on your expertise or target audience's needs.
- Content Creation: Research, organize, and write the content of the e-book, ensuring it is informative, engaging, and well-structured.
- **Formatting and Design:** Format the text, add images or illustrations, and design a visually appealing layout for the e-book.
- **Editing and Proofreading:** Review and revise the content, ensuring accuracy, clarity, and consistency.
- **Conversion and Distribution:** Convert the e-book into popular formats like PDF, ePub, or MOBI and distribute it through online platforms or your own website.

2. **Software Applications:**

- **Concept and Planning:** Identify a problem or need that the software application can address. Outline the features, functionalities, and user experience.

- Design and Prototyping: Create wireframes or mockups to visualize the user interface and user experience (UI/UX) of the application. Iterate on the design based on feedback.
- Development: Write the code and develop the software application using programming languages, frameworks, and tools appropriate for the platform (e.g., web, mobile, desktop).
- Testing and Quality Assurance: Conduct thorough testing to identify and fix bugs, ensure the application functions as intended, and provide a smooth user experience.
- Deployment and Maintenance: Package the application for deployment, release it to the appropriate app stores or platforms, and provide ongoing maintenance and updates.

3. **Online Courses:**

- Course Planning: Determine the learning objectives, structure, and modules for the online course. Define the target audience and their needs.
- Content Creation: Develop the course content, including video lectures, slide presentations, quizzes, assignments, and supplementary materials. Ensure the content is engaging, comprehensive, and aligned with the learning objectives.
- Recording and Production: Record the video lectures using a camera or screen recording software. Edit the videos, add captions or subtitles, and enhance the production quality.
- Learning Management System (LMS) Setup: Choose an LMS platform to host and deliver the course. Set up the course structure, upload the content, and configure access and enrollment options.

- **Testing and Quality Assurance:** Test the course content, interactive elements, and assessments to ensure they function correctly and provide a seamless learning experience.
- **Launch and Support:** Publish the course on the chosen platform and promote it to the target audience. Provide customer support, address queries, and continuously update the course based on feedback.

4.**Digital Art and Graphics:**

- **Ideation and Conceptualization:** Develop ideas and concepts for digital artwork or graphics based on the intended purpose, style, and message.
- **Sketching and Drafting:** Create initial sketches or drafts using traditional or digital tools to outline the composition, shapes, and elements of the artwork.
- **Digital Creation:** Utilize graphics design software (e.g., Adobe Photoshop, Illustrator) or specialized digital art tools (e.g., Procreate) to create the artwork, applying colors, textures, effects, and typography.
- **Refinement and Detailing:** Refine the digital artwork, paying attention to details, proportions, shading, and any required adjustments or revisions.
- **Export and Delivery:** Export the digital artwork in the appropriate format (e.g., JPEG, PNG, vector) for its intended use, such as web graphics, illustrations, or print materials.

These are just a few examples of digital products and their creation processes. The specific steps and tools involved may vary depending on the nature of the digital product and the creator's preferences.

There are several platforms available that can facilitate the sale of digital products. These platforms provide a convenient and secure way to showcase, distribute, and monetize your digital creations. Here are some popular platforms to sell digital products:

1. **Online Marketplaces:**

- **Etsy:** Primarily known for handmade crafts and vintage items, Etsy also allows sellers to offer digital products such as art prints, patterns, e-books, and more.
- **Creative Market:** A marketplace focused on design assets, including fonts, graphics, templates, and themes for web design, branding, and creative projects.
- **Envato Market:** Offers a range of digital products, including themes and templates for websites, graphics, videos, music, plugins, and more.

2. **E-commerce Platforms:**

- **Shopify:** A comprehensive e-commerce platform that enables you to create your own online store and sell digital products along with physical goods.
- **WooCommerce:** A plugin for WordPress websites that allows you to set up a full-featured e-commerce store and sell digital products using various payment gateways.
- **Gumroad:** A platform designed specifically for creators, Gumroad allows you to sell digital products, subscriptions, memberships, and even physical merchandise.

3. **E-learning Platforms:**

- **Udemy:** A popular online learning marketplaces that allows instructors to create and sell online courses on various topics. Udemy handles the hosting, payment processing, and marketing.
- **Teachable:** A platform that enables you to create and sell online courses independently. It provides tools for course creation, customization, marketing, and payment processing.
- **Skillshare:** Focuses on creative and skill-based courses. You can create and publish your courses on Skillshare and earn revenue based on student enrollment.

4. **Self-Hosted Solutions (self-hosted solutions provide complete control and customization over the selling process, but require more technical expertise and setup):**

- **Easy Digital Downloads:** A WordPress plugin that allows you to set up a digital store and sell products like software, e-books, music, and more.
- **Magento:** A robust open-source e-commerce platform that can be customized to sell digital products, offering extensive features for managing and scaling an online store.
- **WooCommerce with Digital Downloads Extensions:** By combining the WooCommerce plugin with digital downloads extensions, you can sell digital products directly from your WordPress website.

These platforms offer varying features, pricing structures, and audiences. Consider factors such as ease of use, payment processing options, licensing and protection mechanisms, marketing capabilities, and fees when choosing the platform that best suits your needs aligns with your digital product offerings.

Here's some guidance on marketing, pricing, and delivering value to customers for your digital products:

1. **Marketing:**

- **Identify Your Target Audience:** Determine who your ideal customers are, their needs, preferences, and where they can be reached. Tailor your marketing efforts accordingly.
- **Develop a Brand Identity:** Create a compelling brand identity that resonates with your target audience. This includes a unique value proposition, visual branding elements, and a consistent brand voice.
- **Content Marketing:** Produce high-quality content related to your digital products. This can include blog posts, videos, podcasts, or social media content that educates, entertains, or solves problems for your target audience. Share your content on relevant platforms and engage with your audience to build relationships.
- **Social Media Marketing:** Leverage social media platforms to promote your digital products. Engage with your audience, share product updates, behind-the-scenes content, customer testimonials, and run targeted advertising campaigns to reach potential customers.
- **Influencer Marketing:** Collaborate with influencers or experts in your niche to showcase your digital products. Their endorsements and reviews can help increase visibility and build credibility.

- **Email Marketing:** Build an email list of interested prospects and customers. Send regular newsletters, exclusive offers, and updates about your digital products to nurture relationships and encourage repeat purchases.

2. **Pricing:**

- **Research the Market:** Understand the market dynamics and competitive landscape for similar digital products. Consider factors such as quality, features, and customer expectations to determine a competitive yet profitable price point.
- **Value-Based Pricing:** Set prices based on the perceived value your digital products provide to customers. Consider the benefits, outcomes, or solutions they offer and align the price with the value proposition.
- **Tiered Pricing:** Offer different pricing tiers or packages for your digital products. Provide additional features, bonuses, or support at higher price points to cater to different customer segments and their willingness to pay.
- **Promotions and Discounts:** Occasionally run promotions or offer discounts to attract new customers, encourage upsells, or reward loyal customers. Ensure the discounts do not undermine the perceived value of your products.

3. **Delivering Value to Customers:**

- **Product Quality:** Ensure your digital products are of high quality, well-designed, and user-friendly. Continuously improve and update them based on customer feedback and evolving market needs.

- **Customer Support:** Provide prompt and helpful customer support to address and inquiries, issues, or technical difficulties customers may encounter. Offer various support channels, such as email, chat, or a dedicated support portal.
- **Clear Instructions and Documentation:** Include detailed instructions or documentation on how to use your digital products effectively. Provide FAQs, tutorials, or video guides to help customers make the most of their purchase.
- **Continuous Improvement:** Actively seek feedback from customers to understand their experiences and areas for improvement. Use this feedback to enhance your digital products, add new features, or address any shortcomings.
- **Bonuses or Extras:** Provide additional value to customers by offering bonuses, exclusive content, templates, or resources that complement or enhance the utility of your digital products.

Marketing, pricing, and delivering value are ongoing processes. Continuously monitor customer feedback, adapt your strategies, and stay responsive to changing market demands to ensure the success of your digital products.

CHAPTER SIX: BLOGGING AND CONTENT MONETIZATION

Blogging is the practice of regularly creating and publishing written content on a website, known as a blog. It involves sharing information, opinions, experiences, or expertise on various topics which can range from personal interests and hobbies to professional niches and industry specific subjects. Blogs typically consist of articles or blog posts that are organized in reverse chronological order. Blogging has gained immense popularity over the years, and it offers significant income potential for those who approach it strategically and dedicate time and effort to building a successful blog. Here are some key aspects to consider regarding the income potential of blogging:

1. **Monetization Methods:**

- **Advertising:** Bloggers can generate income by displaying advertisements on their blogs. This can be through networks like Google AdSense or direct partnerships with advertisers.

- **Affiliate Marketing:** Bloggers can promote products or services through affiliate links, earning commission when readers make a purchase through their referral.
- **Sponsored Content:** Bloggers can collaborate with brands and create sponsored posts or reviews in exchange for compensation.
- **Digital Products:** Bloggers can create and sell their own digital products such as e-books, courses, templates, or digital downloads related to their niche.
- **Membership or Subscription:** Some bloggers offer premium content or access to exclusive resources through membership or subscription models, generating recurring income.

2. **Building an Audience:**

- **Consistent Content Creation:** Regularly publishing high-quality content is crucial for attracting and retaining readers. Consistency helps build a loyal audience.
- **Search Engine Optimization (SEO):** Optimizing blog posts for search engines can increase visibility and organic traffic to the blog.
- **Social Media Promotion:** Leveraging social media platforms to promote blog posts, engage with the audience, and expend the blog's reach.
- **Email Marketing:** Building an email list and sending newsletters with valuable content helps foster a direct connection with readers and drives traffic back to the blog.

3. **Niche Selection and Expertise:**

- Choosing a specific niche or topic of expertise helps establish authority and attract a targeted audience interested in that subject.
- Providing unique insights, valuable information, or solutions to problems within the chosen niche enhances the blog's reputation and increases its income potential.

4. **Networking and Collaboration:**

- Building relationships with other bloggers, industry influencers, or experts can lead to collaboration opportunities, guest posting, or joint ventures, expanding the blog's exposure and potential income streams.

5. **Diversification and Multiple Income Streams:**

- It's advisable to explore multiple monetization methods and not rely solely on one source of income. Diversifying income streams can provide stability and maximize earning potential.

It's important to note that blogging requires consistent effort, time, and dedication. Success and income potential can vary widely depending on factors such as niche competitiveness, quality of content, audience engagement, marketing strategies, and the blogger's commitment to growth.

While blogging can be a lucrative endeavor, it's crucial to set realistic expectations and understand that income may take time to materialize. Building a successful blog requires a long-term commitment, a passion for the chosen niche, and a focus on delivering value to the audience. Let's discuss niche selection, content creation, and search engine optimization (SEO) in more detail:

1. **Niche Selection:**

- **Choose a Specific Topic:** Select a niche that aligns with your interests, expertise, or passion. It should be a specific topic within a broader industry to help you stand out and target a specific audience.
- **Research Market Demand:** Assess the potential audience size and demand for your chosen niche. Look for a balance between audience interest and competition to find a viable niche.
- **Consider Profitability:** Evaluate the income potential of your niche. Research if there are monetization opportunities like affiliate programs, sponsored content, or digital product sales within your chosen niche.

2. **Content Creation:**

- **Understand Your Audience:** Define your target audience's demographics, interests, and pain points. Tailor your content to provide value and address their needs.
- **Develop a Content Strategy:** Plan the types of content you will create, such as informative articles, tutorials, opinion pieces, interviews, or product reviews. Create an editorial calendar to maintain consistency.
- **High-Quality Content:** Focus on delivering well-researched, informative, and engaging content. Use storytelling, visuals, and examples to make your content more compelling.

- **Formatting and Readability:** Structure your content with headings, subheadings, bullet points, and short paragraphs to improve readability. Use relevant images, videos or infographics to enhance visual appeal.
- **Consistency:** Publish content on a regular schedule to keep your audience engaged and attract new visitors. Consistency builds trust and helps search engines recognize your blog as a reliable source of information.

3. **Search Engine Optimization (SEO):**

- **Keyword Research:** Identify relevant keywords and phrases that people use to search for information related to your niche. Use tools like Google Keyword Planner or SEMrush to find popular and less competitive keywords.
- **On-Page Optimization:** Optimize your blog posts by incorporating keywords strategically in the title, headings, URL, meta description, and within the content itself. Ensure your content provides value and matches search intent.
- **Quality Backlinks:** Acquire high-quality backlinks from reputable websites to improve your blog's authority and search engine rankings. This can be done through guest posting, outreach, or creating valuable content that others naturally link to.
- **Site Speed and Mobile Optimization:** Ensure your blog loads quickly and is mobile-friendly. Optimize images, use caching, and choose a reliable hosting provider to improve site speed.
- **User Experience:** Design a user-friendly blog layout with easy navigation, clear categories, and a search function. Make sure your blog is accessible and offers a seamless experience across different devices and browsers.

Regularly monitor your blog's performance, track keyword rankings, analyze traffic sources, and make adjustments to optimize your content for better visibility and organic search traffic. By selecting a niche you're passionate about, consistently creating valuable content, and implementing SEO best practices, you can enhance the visibility of your blog, attract a targeted audience, and ultimately achieve your blogging goals.

There are several monetization strategies you can implement for blogging and content creation. Here are some common ones:

1. **Advertising:**

- **Display Ads:** Join advertising networks like Google AdSense or Media.net to display contextual ads on your blog. You earn revenue based on ad impressions (CPM) or clicks (CPC).
- **Direct Advertising:** Sell ad space directly to advertisers or brands. This can involve placing banner ads, sponsored content, or native advertising on your blog.

2. **Affiliate Marketing:**

- Promote products or services through affiliate links. When a reader clicks on your affiliate link and makes a purchase, you earn a commission. Join affiliate networks like Amazon Associates, ShareASale, or CJ Affiliate, or work directly with individual brands.

3. **Sponsored Content:**

- Collaborate with brands or companies to create sponsored blog posts, reviews, or sponsored social media posts. You receive compensation in exchange for featuring their products or services.

4. **Digital Products:**

- **E-books:** Write and sell e-books on topics relevant to your blog niche. Platforms like Amazon Kindle Direct Publishing or Gumroad can help with distribution.
- **Online Courses:** Create and sell online courses or educational materials related to your expertise or niche. Platforms like Udemy, Teachable, or Thinkific provide tools to host and sell courses.
- **Membership or Subscription:** Offer exclusive content, resources, or a private community for paid members or subscribers. Patreon or WordPress membership plugins can help facilitate this.

5. **Freelancing or Counseling:**

- Leverage your expertise gained from blogging to offer freelance services or consulting in your niche. This can include writing, design, coaching, or advising clients based on your area of expertise.

6. **Events or Workshops:**

- Organize in-person or virtual events, workshops, or seminars related to your blog's niche. Offer tickets or registration to monetize the event through ticket sales or sponsorships.

7. Donations:

- Include a donation button or set up a platform like Ko-fi or Buy Me a Coffee to allow readers to support your blog by making voluntary donations.

8. Brand Partnerships and Sponsorships:

- Collaborate with brands on sponsored content, brand ambassadorships, or long-term partnerships. This can involve promoting their products or services through blog posts, social media, or dedicated campaigns.

9. Adapting to Emerging Trends:

- Stay updated on emerging trends and new monetization opportunities. This can include exploring podcasting, video content creation, selling merchandise, or offering consulting services through platforms like Clarity.fm.

It's important to choose monetization strategies that align with your audience's interests and preferences. Be transparent and disclose any paid or sponsored content to maintain trust with your readers. Experiment with different strategies, track performance, and optimize your approach based on what works best for your blog and audience.

Growing your traffic, engaging your audience, and building a brand through your blog and content creation is important to your success. Focus on creating content that is informative, unique, and relevant to your target audience's interests and needs. Offer actionable tips, insights, or solutions to their problems. Use storytelling, visuals, and examples to make your content more engaging and relatable. Conduct thorough research, cite credible sources, and strive for accuracy and professionalism in your content.

Implement SEO best practices to improve your blog's visibility in search engine results. Conduct keyword research, optimize meta tags, headings, and content, and build quality backlinks. Aim to provide content that matches search intent, answering the questions or needs of users searching for relevant topics. Regularly monitor and analyze your SEO performance using tools like Google Analytics or SEMrush.

Actively promote your blog and content across various channels. Share your posts on social media platforms, engage with your audience, and encourage sharing and discussion. Participate in relevant online communities, forums, or social media groups related to your niche. Share your expertise, answer questions, and establish yourself as a valuable resource. Consider collaborating with other bloggers or influencers in your niche for cross-promotion and exposure.

Build and email list to promote your blog. Offer valuable incentives like e-books, exclusive content, or resources in exchange for readers subscribing to your email list. Send regular newsletters with updates, new content releases, or special offers to keep your audience engaged and encourage repeat visits to your blog.

Engage with your audience by responding to comments and messages promptly. Encourage discussion and interaction on your blog and social media platforms. Ask questions, conduct surveys, or run polls to gather feedback and insights from your audience. Consider hosting live Q&A sessions, webinars, or AMAs (Ask Me Anything) to directly engage with your audience in real-time.

Seek opportunities to collaborate with other bloggers or influencers in your niche. This can involve guest posting on their blogs, hosting joint webinars or podcasts, or participating in roundup posts. Guest posting allows you to reach a new audience and build backlinks to your blog, improving your visibility and authority.

Consistently publish new content on a regular schedule to keep your audience engaged and encourage return visits. Develop an editorial calendar to plan and organize your content creation process. Be authentic and build a brand identity that reflects your values, personality, and niche expertise. Stay true to your authentic voice and maintain transparency with your audience. Consistently deliver value, be reliable, and build trust with your readers.

Regularly analyze your blog's performance using analytics tools. Track metrics such as traffic, engagement, and conversion rates. Identify trends, patterns, and content preferences of your audience to adapt your content strategy and focus on what resonates the most. Stay committed, adapt to feedback, and continuously improve your content and engagement strategies to cultivate a loyal and engaged audience.

CHAPTER SEVEN: ONLINE COACHING AND CONSULTING

The demand for online coaching and consulting services has been growing rapidly in recent years. Online coaching and consulting services provide a high level of convenience to clients. They can access expert guidance and support from the comfort of their own homes or offices, without the need to travel or schedule in-person meetings. This flexibility appeals to individuals with busy schedules or those who live in remote areas.

Online services have no geographical limitations. Clients can connect with coaches and consultants from anywhere in the world, allowing them to access specialized expertise that may not be available locally. This global reach expands the pool of potential clients for coaches and consultants, creating more opportunities for both parties. They often have lower overhead costs compared to traditional in-person services. Coaches and consultants can eliminate expenses associated with renting office spaces, commuting, or providing physical materials. This cost-effectiveness can translate into more affordable services for clients or allow professionals to offer competitive pricing.

Online services can be structured to accommodate clients' specific needs, making efficient use of their time. Clients can schedule sessions at their convenience, minimizing disruptions to their daily routines. Additionally, virtual communication tools facilitate quick and seamless interactions, reducing the time spent on administrative tasks and enabling more focused and productive sessions. These services attract professionals with specialized knowledge in various fields. Clients can access experts who offer tailored guidance in specific areas such as business, career development, personal growth, health and wellness, financial planning, and more. This targeted expertise can help clients achieve their goals more effectively.

Some clients prefer the anonymity provided by online coaching and consulting services. They may feel more comfortable discussing personal or sensitive topics without the fear of being recognized in a public setting. Online platforms often offer secure and private communication channels, fostering a confidential environment for clients. Advancements in technology have allowed this to happen. Anonymous and confidential communication is possible through instant messaging, file-sharing platforms, emailing, etc.

Overall, the demand for online coaching and consulting services stems from the desire for convenience, global access to expertise, cost-effectiveness, time efficiency, specialized guidance, confidentiality, and advancements in technology. As the digital landscape continues to expand, it is expected that the demand for these services will continue to grow.

Niche selection and identifying target clients are crucial steps in establishing and growing a successful online coaching and consulting business. Here are some reasons why these aspects are important:

- **Focus and Expertise:** Choosing a specific niche allows you to focus your efforts and become an expert in that particular area. By specializing in a niche, you can develop a deep understanding of the challenges, needs, and opportunities within that market. This expertise helps you differentiate yourself from generalists and positions you as a valuable resource for clients seeking assistance in that specific area.
- **Effective Marketing and Messaging:** When you know your target clients and their specific needs, you can craft your marketing messages to resonate with them. By tailoring your communication to address their plan points and aspirations, you increase the chances of attracting their attention and conveying the value you can provide. Understanding your target clients' language, preferences, and motivations enables you to develop marketing strategies that are more likely to generate leads and conversions.
- **Enhanced Client Relationships:** Identifying your target clients allows you to establish deeper connections with them. When you understand their unique circumstances, challenges, and goals, you can offer tailored solutions, and personalized support. This level of customization fosters trust, builds stronger relationships, and increases client satisfaction and loyalty.

- **Competitive Advantage:** In a crowded online coaching and consulting marketplace, differentiating yourself is essential. By selecting a niche, you can position yourself as a specialist and stand out from the competition. Clients often prefer working with professionals who have a deep understanding of their specific needs and can provide highly relevant guidance. This competitive advantage increases your chances of attracting clients and building a reputation as a go-to expert in your chosen niche.
- **Efficient Resource Allocation:** Targeting a specific audience allows you to optimize your resources effectively. By focusing your marketing efforts, content creation, and service offerings on a specific niche, you can allocate your time, energy, and resources more efficiently. This targeted approach helps you maximize your impact and generate better results with the resources at your disposal.
- **Referral and Word-of-Mouth Potential:** When you specialize in a niche, satisfied clients are more likely to refer you to others who have similar needs. Positive word-of-mouth referrals can be a powerful source of new clients for your online coaching or consulting business. By serving a specific target audience exceptionally well, you increase the likelihood of clients recommending your services to others within the same niche.

Niche selection and identifying target clients are critical for online coaching and consulting services. They allow you to focus your expertise, tailor your marketing efforts, establish deeper client relationships, gain a competitive advantage, allocate resources efficiently, and generate referral opportunities. By understanding and serving a specific target audience, you can position yourself as an expert in your niche and attract clients who are most likely to benefit from and value your services.

When it comes to packaging and pricing your online coaching consulting services, it's essential to consider various factors to ensure your offerings align with your target clients' needs and provide value. Clearly define the specific services you will offer. Identify the outcomes or benefits your clients can expect from working with you. Break down your services into different packages or tiers based on the level of support, duration, or intensity of engagement.

Research and analyze the market rates for similar services in your niche. Understand the pricing ranges and models used by other professionals offering online coaching and consulting services. This research will give you a sense of industry standards and help you position your pricing competitively. Take into account your expertise, qualifications, and years of experience. The level of knowledge and the value you bring to the table should be reflected in your pricing. Clients are often willing to pay a premium for experts with a proven track record or specialized expertise.

Focus on the value you deliver to clients rather than simply charging based on your time or effort. Consider the impact your services can have on your clients' lives or businesses and price accordingly. This approach allows you to capture the value your clients receive and ensures your pricing is commensurate with the results you help them achieve. Create different service packages or tiers to cater to different client needs and budgets. This could include options such as one-on-one coaching, group coaching, self-paced programs, or VIP intensives. Each package should clearly outline what is included, such as the number of sessions, additional resources, or ongoing support.

Collect testimonials and success stories from past clients to demonstrate the value and impact of your services. Displaying social proof can help justify your pricing and build trust with potential clients. Testimonials can highlight the tangible outcomes clients have achieved by working with you. Consider offering different pricing options to accommodate clients with varying budgets or requirements. This could involve providing payment plans, discounted packages for long-term commitments, or introductory offers for new clients. Offering flexibility and scalability in your pricing can help attract a wider range of clients.

Regularly review and assess your pricing strategy. As your experience, expertise, and market demand grow, you may need to adjust your pricing accordingly. Monitor client feedback, track the effectiveness of your services, and stay updated with market trends to ensure your pricing remains competitive and reflects the value you provide. Remember that finding the right pricing strategy may require some experimentation and adaptation. It's important to strike a balance between charging what you're worth and ensuring your services are accessible to your target audience. Regularly evaluate and refine your pricing strategy based on client feedback, market conditions, and your business goals to ensure a sustainable and profitable online coaching and consulting practice.

To effectively market your online coaching and consulting services, establish credibility, and deliver value to your clients, you must deliver a strong online presence. Create a professional website that clearly communicates your expertise, services, and value proposition. Optimize your website for search engines to increase visibility. Establish profiles on relevant social media platforms and engage with your target audience through informative and valuable content.

Consistently produce high-quality content that educates and provides value to your target clients. This can include blog posts, articles, videos, podcasts, or infographics. Share your expertise, address common challenges, and offer actionable insights. Promote your content through various channels to reach a wider audience. Position yourself as a thought leader in your niche by sharing your unique insights and perspectives. Publish guest posts on reputable platforms, participate in relevant industry events, or contribute to podcasts and webinars. This enhances your credibility and visibility in the field, attracting potential clients.

Request testimonials from satisfied clients and showcase them on your website and marketing materials. Highlight specific results or transformations clients have experienced through your coaching or consulting. Additionally, create case studies that demonstrate how you've helped clients overcome challenges and achieve their goals. Building relationships with other professionals in your field or related industries is also a great way to market your services. Collaborate on projects, co-create content, or participate in joint webinars or events. Networking and partnerships expand your reach, provide cross-promotion opportunities, and establish credibility through association with trusted individuals or organizations.

Develop a strong brand identity that reflects your expertise, values, and unique selling points. Use consistent branding elements such as logos, colors, and messaging across all your marketing materials. A cohesive and professional brand image enhances credibility and makes a lasting impression on clients. Stay updated with industry trends, research, and best practices. Invest in your own professional development through relevant courses, certifications, or attending conferences. Demonstrating a commitment to learning and growth enhances your expertise and credibility as a coach or consultant.

Prioritize personalized and tailored solutions for your clients. Understand their unique needs, goals, and challenges, and design customized strategies to address them effectively. Offer individualized attention, support, and guidance, ensuring that your clients feel heard and valued. Emphasize the outcomes and results your clients can achieve through your services. Clearly communicate the value they can expect and the specific goals you can help them accomplish. Track progress, provide feedback, and celebrate milestones to showcase the tangible value you deliver.

Offer continuous support beyond the coaching or consulting sessions. Provide resources, tools, or materials that clients can access between sessions to reinforce their learning and progress. Offer email or messaging support to address questions or concerns. This ongoing support demonstrates your commitment to their success. Consistently delivering value, establishing credibility, and effective marketing go hand in hand. By providing exceptional service and demonstrating your expertise, you can build a strong reputation, attract new clients, and cultivate long-term relationships based on trust and results.

CHAPTER EIGHT: PASSIVE INCOME STREAMS AND INVESTMENTS

Passive income refers to income generated with minimal effort or active involvement on the part of the recipient. In the online space, there are several passive income opportunities available. Here are a few popular ones:

- **Dividend Investing:** Dividend investing involves purchasing shares of dividend-paying stocks or funds. As an investor, you receive regular dividend payments, typically quarterly, based on the number of shares you own. Dividend investing can provide a steady stream of income, especially if you invest in companies with a history of consistent dividend payouts.
- **Real Estate Crowdfunding:** Real estate crowdfunding platforms allow individuals to invest in real estate projects alongside other investors. By pooling funds, investors can access real estate opportunities that may have been otherwise out of reach. The platform manages the property, and investors receive a share of the rental income or profits from property sales.

- **Peer-to-Peer Lending:** Peer-to-peer lending platforms connect borrowers with lenders. As a lender, you can lend money to individuals or businesses and earn interest on your investment. These platforms typically have a range of risk levels and interest rates, allowing you to diversify your lending portfolio.
- **Affiliate Marketing:** Affiliate marketing involves promoting products or services through your online platform (e.g., website, blog, social media) and earning a commission for every sale or referral you generate. This can be done through affiliate networks or direct partnerships with businesses. With a well-established platform and targeted audience, affiliate marketing can generate passive income over time.
- **Creating and Selling Digital Products:** If you have specialized knowledge or skills, you can create digital products like e-books, online courses, stock photos, software, or templates. Once created, these products can be sold repeatedly without much additional effort. Platforms like Udemy, Teachable, or Etsy provide marketplaces for selling digital products.
- **Stock Market Investing:** Investing in stocks or exchange-traded funds (ETFs) can be a way to generate passive income if you focus on companies that pay dividends or appreciate value over time. While investing in the stock market can be subject to volatility, long-term investing strategies can generate passive income through dividends and capital gains.
- **Royalties from Intellectual Property:** If you have creative works like books, music, artwork, or software, you can earn royalties by licensing or selling the rights to your work. Platforms like Amazon Kindle Direct Publishing, Shutterstock, or app stores provide opportunities to monetize intellectual property.

It's important to note that while these opportunities have the potential for passive income, they may require some initial effort and ongoing monitoring. Investing always carries a degree of risk, so it's crucial to do thorough research and consider your risk tolerance before committing to any investment strategy. Here are the pros and cons of each option listed:

1. **Dividend Investing: Pros:**

- Regular income: Dividend payments provide a consistent stream of income
- Potential for capital appreciation: Dividend-paying stocks can also appreciate in value, increasing your overall return.
- Diversification: You can invest in a variety of dividend stocks to diversify your portfolio.

Cons:

- Market risk: Dividend stocks are still subject to market fluctuations and can experience price volatility.
- Dividend cuts: Companies may reduce or eliminate their dividend payments, impacting your income.
- Dependency on company performance: Dividend payouts depend on the financial health and profitability of the companies you invest in.

2. **Real Estate Crowdfunding: Pros:**

- Access to real estate investments: Crowdfunding allows you to invest in real estate with lower capital requirements and without the need for direct property ownership.

- **Diversification:** You can invest in multiple properties across different locations or types, reducing risk.
- **Professional management:** The platform handles property management and maintenance tasks.

Cons:

- **Illiquid investments:** Real estate investments can be less liquid compared to other assets, meaning it may take time to convert your investment into cash.
- **Market risk:** Real estate values can fluctuate, impacting the potential returns.
- **Platform risk:** The success of your investment relies on the credibility and competence of the crowdfunding platform.

3. **Peer-to-Peer Lending: Pros:**

- **Higher interest rates:** Peer-to-peer lending can offer higher interest rates compared to traditional savings accounts or bonds.
- **Diversification:** You can spread your investments across multiple loans to mitigate default risk.
- **Direct lending:** You have more control over which borrowers you lend to and can assess their creditworthiness.

Cons:

- **Default risk:** There is a possibility of borrowers defaulting on their loans, leading to potential loss of principal.

- **Lack of regulatory protection:** Peer-to-peer lending may not be subject to the same regulatory safeguards as traditional banking institutions.
- **Platform risk:** The success of your investments is tied to the platform's ability to manage loan origination, collections, and overall risk.

4. Affiliate Marketing: Pros:

- **Low upfront costs:** Affiliate marketing often requires minimal investment to get started.
- **Passive income potential:** Once set up, your affiliate links can generate income without ongoing effort.
- **Flexibility:** You can choose products or services that align with your interests or target audience.

Cons:

- **Dependence on audience and traffic:** Your earnings are reliant on the size and engagement of your audience.
- Market saturation: Some niches may be highly competitive, making it harder to stand out and generate significant income.
- **Affiliate program limitations:** Some affiliate programs have restrictions on promotional methods, payment thresholds, or geographic limitations.

5. Creating and Selling Digital Products: Pros:

- **Scalability:** Digital products can be sold to a large number of customers without incurring additional production costs.

- **Passive income potential:** Once created, digital products can generate income repeatedly without significant effort.
- **Intellectual property ownership:** You retain control and ownership over your creations.

Cons:

- **Upfront time and effort:** Creating high-quality digital products requires initial investment in time and skills.
- **Market competition:** Depending on the niche, there may be intense competition in the digital product marketplace.
- **Marketing and promotion:** Selling digital products requires effective marketing and promotion to reach potential customers.

6. Stock Market Investing: Pros:

- **Potential for capital appreciation:** Investing in stocks can generate returns through both dividends and the growth of share prices.
- **Liquidity:** Stocks are generally more liquid compared to other investment options, allowing you to convert your investments into cash relatively easily.
- **Access to diverse markets:** Stock market investments provide exposure to a wide range of industries and companies.

Cons:

- **Market volatility:** Stock prices can be highly volatile, subjecting your investments to potential losses.

- **Requires research and analysis:** Successful stock market investing often requires a good understanding of the companies and market trends.
- **Risk of individual company performance:** Investing in individual stocks carries the risk of specific companies underperforming or going bankrupt.

7. Royalties from Intellectual Property: Pros:

- **Passive income potential:** Once your intellectual property is created, you can earn royalties without active involvement.
- **Scalability:** Digital platforms allow you to reach a global audience, potentially increasing your income opportunities.
- **Control over your creations:** You retain ownership and control over how your intellectual property is used.

Cons:

- **Intellectual property infringement:** There is a risk of unauthorized use or piracy, which can affect your royalty income.
- **Market demand and competition:** The success of your intellectual property depends on its market appeal and competition in the industry.
- **Initial investment:** Creating high-quality intellectual property may require upfront investment in time, skills, or equipment.

It's important to consider these pros and cons, assess your risk tolerance, and conduct thorough research before choosing any passive income opportunity or investment strategy. Diversification and a long-term perspective are generally advisable to mitigate risk and maximize potential returns.

Risk management is important for any investments and passive income streams. Understand your risk tolerance and assess your willingness and ability to tolerate investment risks. Consider factors such as your financial goals, time horizon, and personal circumstances. Define your objectives and align your investments accordingly to set clear investment goals. For example, if you're seeking income, focus on assets with steady cash flows. If you're aiming for growth, consider investments with higher potential returns but also higher volatility. Diversify your portfolio by spreading your investments across different asset classes, industries, and geographic regions. Diversification helps reduce the impact of any single investment's performance on your overall portfolio. Monitor your portfolio regularly to ensure it aligns with your investment goals and risk tolerance. Rebalance periodically by adjusting the allocation of your investments to maintain diversification.

Thoroughly research and understand the specific passive income opportunity or investment you're considering. Study the mechanics, associated risks, historical performance, and potential returns. Conduct due diligence by researching the companies, platforms, or individuals involved in the investment. Review their track record, financial health, reputation, and regulatory compliance. Look for reviews or feedback from other investors. Keep up with relevant news, market trends, and economic indicators that may affect your investments. Subscribe to reputable financial publications, follow industry experts, and utilize reliable sources of information. Consider consulting with financial advisors or professionals who specialize in the specific investment area you're interested in. They can provide guidance based on their expertise and help you make informed decisions.

Consider diversifying your portfolio across stocks, bonds, real estate, and other asset classes. Each asset class has different risk and return characteristics, which can help balance your overall portfolio. Choose investments with varied risk profiles. Within each asset class, select investments that have different risk levels. This diversifies your exposure within the asset class and helps mitigate the impact of any single investment's performance. Don't rely on a single income stream. Build multiple streams of passive income to reduce dependence on a single income source. This can help safeguard against potential; disruptions or fluctuations in one particular income stream. Regularly review your portfolio's diversification and make adjustments as needed. As market conditions change or your financial goals evolve, rebalance your portfolio to maintain an appropriate level of diversification.

No investment is entirely risk-free and even passive income opportunities require active monitoring and management. It's crucial to tailor your risk management, research, and diversification strategies to your individual circumstances and financial goals.

CONCLUSION

Now is the time to take action and pursue your online income goals. The digital landscape offers endless opportunities for you to tap into your passions, skills, and creativity to create a sustainable income stream. Don't let fear or doubt hold you back. Embrace the power of the internet, where geographical boundaries no longer restrict your potential. Dedicate yourself to learning, growing, and exploring different avenues to find the one that resonates with you. Take small steps every day, building your online presence, honing your skills, and connecting with like-minded individuals. Remember, success may not come overnight, but with persistence, determination, and a willingness to adapt, you can achieve your online income goals and unlock the freedom and flexibility that an online career can provide. Start today and embark on a journey of financial independence and fulfillment.

BRAINSTORM BUSINESS IDEAS